BOOK TITLE:

MY 30 DIVINE

HEARTWARMING

POEMS

WRITTEN BY: (CRYSTAL) YEHUWDIYTH Y. YISRAEL

DEDICATION:

I dedicated this book here first to my Heavenly Father; God, YAHWA, YHWH, MR.LOVE HIMSELF; then to you all out there in the world at large, because he is the reason why I can bring forth this wonderful work of art from the heart with love, in short, this is all made possible; also, accessible to you all, because of him and because of his skills that he has bestowed upon me; for that I am very grateful; as well, I am extremely thankful too.

ACKNOWLEDGEMENT:

I would like to give all thanksgiving, honor, and laudation unto my

Heavenly Father, YAHWA, YHWH, the God of Love; of Heaven,

because he first blessed me with the skills and with the ability

and with the capacity; also, capability to be able to perform this

divine work here with his supreme wisdom, knowledge and with

his amazing and infinite understanding with love. And for that I

will forever be humbly grateful; also, will be extremely

happy to say that all of this here is all made possible he made it

all come to life by breathing his breath of life, love, and light into

me (my mind and spirit); further, giving me the power to craft

this beautiful book of poems here with a happy heart; further,

with a willing spirit to spread these seeds of love and of life throughout the world at large with my freewill. Bottom line, I am

thrilled to do so; to let the world know that. For he is the driving

force behind all good, and perfect gifts. So, let us all give him his

praises, flowers, and props always.

TABLE OF CONTENTS:

The winter

Get your house in order

Dry your eyes

Learn to be patient

The inner you

Look out your window today

Watch your every move

A glass house

Go and smell the roses

Plant your seeds

Repent

Danger is ahead

Stay focus on the most high

Real talk

The sun rises

TAKE A MOMENT

Take a moment.

To breathe.

To exhale.

To stretch.

To think.

To appreciate those that care for you a great deal.

To be real.

To heal.

To mend what is broken.

To enjoy life and to laugh.

And, to love and to live.

Most of all, take a moment to give thanks for all things to the Creator above.

Further, to be grateful, humble and to reflect on all things; that's whether it be good or bad.

And make a sound decision, or choice to be positive, peaceful, productive, pleasant; wise and to rise above all your obstacles; or challenges that the enemy, or life's circumstances may throw at you; or towards your way in any day, or night.

Well, at the end of the day; as I close out, I would like to say, take a moment to be right in thought, in actions; also, in dealings and in your words, steps; or in the hand that you seek to play, and let it be displayed on all occasions.

Bottom line,

Take a moment to sort things out before you make your final move.

Always remember it's not always how you start, but it is always how you end, whatever it is, that matters the most.

So, in most cases, it is not always the first impression that does that most damage, but at times, it is the last impression that makes the lasting impact; or expression, or mark.

Anyway, either way, it goes, let your starting point; or your ending point be good, great; or a wonderful one; that way you can't lose, but win at the end; or at the beginning.

And so, with that, being said, take a moment to see things (the Truth) clear without fear.

LOL...

Oh, my dear, this is where I end.

Shalom, Shalom!

Poem written by: Crystal da rock/ Yehuwdiyth Y. Yisrael.

MAKE YOUR DAY BRIGHT

Make your day bright.

With the right stuff.

And with the right minds around you.

Bottom line,

Make your day bright and out sight

With lots of love and laughter; with real positive energy and thoughts.

Hey... All you need is you experiencing being and feeling good, right and

dynamite deep down inside; all will be bright.

For it is you that determines how your day begins and ends, despite who,

or what is around you, or me.

Poem written by: Crystal da rock/ Yehuwdiyth Y. Yisrael

BREAK THE CYCLE

Break the cycle.

That recycle hate.

That takes away your greatness.

That is impeding your growth.

And that is changing your positivity into negativity.

Further,
Break the cycle.

That is riding you like a bicycle.

And, again, I say break the cycle

That is affecting your present; that will change your future, not for the better.

And that's under any circumstances; or weather.

Bottom line,

Break the cycle just so, you can let the cycle, or the circle of life, love, light, and laughter continue to shine through; makes things brighter, stronger, and more and more and fonder; while it lasts longer with the right elements, attitudes and with the right mindset.

So, loves, always remember that it is the desire; the mindset behind the cycle that needs to be broken and not to be taken as a token at all.

And so, with that being said,

Give it all that you have, love and stand firm and tall; don't stall or fall when it comes to breaking the cycle.

Praise Love, the Gods, and the Goddesses of Love and of righteousness above always.

Poem written by: Crystal da rock/ Yehuwdiyth Y. Yisrael.

<u>SERVING GOD</u>

Serving God,

is actually serving goodness.

Serving compassion.

It's serving righteousness.

It's serving love.

Also, It is serving, everything, that is beneficial to the mind, heart, spirit, and the soul needs.

It's a deed that is out of this world; that comes with extraordinary wisdom, knowledge, strength, peace and with an infinite and divine understanding that supersedes all earthly wisdom, knowledge and understanding.

In fact, it's something that requires great skills, thrill and will; that is done with soundness of mind, a happy heart and with a humbling spirit sincerely and wholeheartedly.

So, bottom line loves, serving God, Mr. Love Himself, is having a pure heart.

For it is the pureness of everything; the willingness to serve him, and who he is that makes God, our Heavenly Father smile and happy too.

Shalom.

Poem written by: Crystal da rock/ Yehuwdiyth Y. Yisrael.

KEEP YOUR LIGHT ON

Keep your light on.

At all times.

Simply, because with it on, it can help keep you from falling into a ditch.

Also, it will stop you from being trapped; or from accepting any foolishness that comes in any form.

And, further, keep your light on,
Because it will bring you bliss and happiness; not distress or stress.

Bottom line,
Keep your light on, because that way darkness cannot consume you, or your mind.

And, besides that, it is important to do, because keeping the lights on can only help make things better and brighter, whether the situations are big or small.

All in all,
Lights on means feeling better; being in a greater state of mind without being blind or behind.

So, love, in all you do, move with caution; always keep your lights on while you take your steps; or make your moves.

Shalom.

Poem written by: Crystal da rock/ Yehuwdiyth Y. Yisrael.

A HOT CUP OF TEA

A hot cup of tea.

It's refreshing.

It's soothing.

It's something that does wonders for the mind, body, spirit.

It's organic.

It's also something that you and I can enjoy at home alone, at the cafe, or by the sea.

Bottom line,

A hot cup of delicious tea can help keep the stress away, or at bay; while, at the time, it makes you feel warm, happy, blessed; also, very divine deep down inside.

Well, folks, I'm heading to the kitchen right now to go sip on mine. LOL...

Poem written by: Crystal da rock/ Yehuwdiyth Y. Yisrael.

KEEP A RECORD OF

Keep a record of
What is important.

Meaningful, beautiful; also, of the things that will help you, heal you, keep
you and that will challenge you; of the things, people, faces, memories,
dreams, of energy that will help uplift you, stimulate you, complement
you; also, that will help build you up and bring you to your highest peak,
potential and positivity.

But most importantly,
Keep a record of what the Almighty God do; does in your mind; also in
your heart, spirit, and soul. For those are moments of gold; a beauty to
always behold.

And that way, at the end of the day,
You can when you need it, it will always be there to go back to; or to refer
to.

Shalom.

Poem written by: Crystal da rock/ Yehuwdiyth Y. Yisrael.

<u>TODAY</u>

Today presented

Itself as to be gray all day.

And it presented itself with some rain, but it

didn't cause any pain; nor did I complain.

Further, it presented itself to be cold; breezy.

Also, it presented itself with the wind hollering; swishing throughout in

between the tall buildings, and near the windows of my room.

And no, I was not doomed.

If anything, I kind of like it.

Today I saw; seen the day to be beautiful; also, really amazing despite of

the fact, that it wasn't a sunny day, but to me, the fact remained, that I was

blessed to see it, experienced and to even enjoyed it through and by the

Creator's love, grace, and compassion.

And for that I am super grateful for it all; all in all.

And so, loves, let us all remember to give thanks to the Creator above, for everything; that's whether it is something that we expected or not.

For he knows best when it is all said and done
LOL...

Poem written by: Crystal da rock/ Yehuwdiyth Y. Yisrael.

FOLLOW YOUR HEART

Follow your heart.

When it leads you to something right.

When it makes you feel happy.

Bottom line,

Follow your heart with all soundness; that way it will not be all based on

emotions only, but with the foundation being logic and rationality.

For the heart can at times be a deceitful device.

Shalom.

Poem written by: Crystal da rock/ Yehuwdiyth Y. Yisrael

THE MEAL YOU FIX TODAY

Let it be good.

Let it be sweet.

With a touch of heat.

And make it a good treat.

Make it taste great, delicious, and yummy
for every tummy.

Bottom line,
Make it something that no one will forget; nor you will regret.

In a nutshell,

Let the meal you make be something that will soothe; fulfill the mind,

heart, body, spirit, and the soul of course; that is filled with the fruits of

the tree of life; that is whether it be mentally, spiritually; or physically.

Overall, just let it be divine with the touch of Love, joy, and peace.

Shalom, shalom; praise Love, the Gods, and the Goddesses of Love
always and forevermore.

Poem written by: Crystal da rock/ Yehuwdiyth Y. Yisrael.

BILLS

Bills.

It has a very popular name; further, is a very famous commodity, that if we're not careful it would send us insane.

And it, bill that is, has no shame.

And that's whether you have fame; or are lame.

Still, bill still plays the same hand, gives you his only option, which is to pay him off while he plays the same game.

And boy! I tell you... bill doesn't mess around every time he comes around.

He wants to make sure that he leaves with the title; or with the championship belt, while he makes us yelp; or makes us scream for help.

LOL...

Well, anyway, as I close out, I will say no matter what bill, or the thing called bills always seeks to win at the end; that's whether you're high or low.

Bottom line,

Bills always come out with a knockout blow to take you down, keep you with a frown; or to steal your joy and crown.

LOL...

But hey all I can say is you live and you learn, a way to not let it swallow you in whole; or to put you in a hole.

LOL.... Just find a way to at least stay on top of your game; of what you have gained and maintain; keep bill, or the bills in a short leash.

Shalom my loves, and just consider using wisdom in your every move you make; in every step that you take; also, in your every thought that you think, just so you won't sink; or be overtaken by this thing called bills.

Ha! Ha! Ha! Ha!

Poem written by: Crystal da rock/ Yehuwdiyth Y. Yisrael.

<u>UNITE</u>

Unite.

It's about you and me.

Again, I say unite.

Because it will bring togetherness and excitement.

Furthermore,

I say unite, because it will be helpful; also, you will not be alone; or

without a team.

Bottom line,

Unite, because uniting for what's right and standing in unity with sincerity

for truth, peace, love, and righteousness is worth fighting for and living

for.

For unity with a good cause and for a good cause is something to do,

cherish; not let perish always.

So, unite my love(s) with love, wisdom, knowledge and with a great understanding within your hearts, minds and within your spirits without a doubt.

For this is what God, Mr. Love Himself; his heavenly host would want and be thrilled about.

So, shalom and praise Love, the Gods, and the Goddesses of Love and of righteousness always and forevermore.

Poem written by: Crystal da rock/ Yehuwdiyth Y. Yisrael.

STAY CONNECTED

Stay connected.

To what is true to you.

Because that is what matters the most.

And that is the best way to go.

And, that there is whether it's high or low.

Always stay connected mentally and spiritually; as well, emotionally balanced; further, be true to yourself; to everyone that means you well, and not hell.

But most of all, stay connected to the highest, the Creator and our Heavenly Father always; wholeheartedly and totally.

For this is the most important connection above all.

Praise Love, the God of Love always and forevermore.

Poem written by: Crystal da rock/ Yehuwdiyth Y. Yisrael.

SEEK THE TRUTH

Seek the truth.

For it is the way and the life,
That the Creator above wants us to take and to embrace in real haste.

Why?
Because it is what will help set and make us free in any way, any day, plus
in a good way.

Bottom line,
Seek the truth,
Because it is the greatest gift of all things; that this is what will help save
us, heal; bless us in a way that nothing else can; or will bless us, groom
us; or elevate us.

And so, with that being said,
Always seek the King's Dome first; his righteousness and watch and see
everything else (that you are lacking, like the superior and divine wisdom,
knowledge and understanding of the God of Love and of Heaven above)
be added unto you abundantly.

In a nutshell,

I say that (which is seek the truth), because it is priceless, precious; also, is very powerful; incredible and greatly beneficial to; for our mind, spirit, heart; also, to our soul as well.

Thank the Highest, our Father of Heaven for the Truth and for his love, grace, and mercy.

Poem written by: Crystal da rock/ Yehuwdiyth Y. Yisrael.

I say that (which is seek the truth), because it is priceless, precious; also,

CALMNESS

Calmness.

It's something that is beneficial.

It's a way to relax.

It's something that we need to enjoy, experience; even to cherish.

Why?
Because it benefits our mind, heart, spirit, and even the soul as well.

Bottom line,
It's a blessing; it's an ability to experience peace; tranquility; not stress or distress.

So, love stays calm no matter what happens; that's no matter where you are at.

Just practice being calm; or showing calmness in the time it is needed the most.

For this is where the activation starts; or begins.

Shalom.

Poem written by: Crystal da rock/ Yehuwdiyth Y. Yisrael.

THE WINTER

The winter.

It's a time of the year

When it is very cold.

And it's a time when it causes us to want to be warm and cozy.

And it's the time where we enjoy our baked goods, delicious foods, and

nice hot chocolate.

As a matter of fact,

It's a time that I enjoy, especially the coolness of it, the winter that is, and

that's without the wind blowing.

Further,

I like winter, because it's another gift, another option, and another offer

that the good Lord, Mr. Love Himself, has blessed us with to enjoy when

all the other seasons have ended.

And so, with that, pull out your coats, jackets and mittens, hats, and scarves; while you enjoy; experience the winter with a warm heart, spirit; smile for a little while.

Shalom.

Poem written: Crystal da rock/Yehuwdiyth Y. Yisrael.

GET YOUR HOUSE IN ORDER

Get your house in order.

Why? Because it is a great way to live.

Also, it is because it helps to make it easier to keep things aligned.

Again,

Get your house in order because a

house in order is like heaven.

Further,

It's like a place, a space; or an atmosphere that is without the leaven.

As a matter of fact,

Getting your house in order is like putting things into perspective.

Also, it means getting your thoughts together; cleaning anything that

doesn't belong; that is wrong.

Well, bottom line,

Getting your house in order simply means getting you, your mind, heart;

spirit right; also, in accord with the Creator above with love and with

good

Understanding that

Getting your house in order is a must; a plus that will continue to bring much bliss and happiness for you, your family; for anyone that sees; that also understands the vision.

Shalom, enjoy your day and your time, life with peace always.

Poem written by: Crystal da rock/ Yehuwdiyth Y. Yisrael.

DRY YOUR EYES

Dry your eyes.

And realize that crying can't; won't solve everything.

Although, it's okay to cry sometimes, because it helps you and me to release some pressure.

But, at the end of the day, as I close out, I would like to say,

Dry your eyes and seek to pray; also, to take action to help bring about some real beautiful changes, options and solutions that will help keep the crying, the sobbing, and the helpless feeling away; at bay, and to help make room for joy and happiness to come to play without a delay.

And, that way, the thought of me saying dry your eyes can be a thing of the past.

LOL...

Shalom.

Poem written by: Crystal da rock/ Yehuwdiyth Y. Yisrael.

LEARN TO BE PATIENT

Learn to be patient.

Because it will pay off in the end.

Because it will prepare you in a way to be ready for when the time comes

to perform it, display it; also, to manifest it at the most needed moment.

And remember that patience is a virtue.

Bottom line,

It's important to be patient because it's a beautiful quality.

Also, it can help keep you and me out of any unnecessary situations,

conditions, or problems.

And so, with that, being said,

Seek to be patient if you are not; if you are patient, then seek to be eager

as well, just so, complacency won't settle in, but to gain and obtain;

further maintain a balance between being patient and impatient.

Shalom, shalom and have a wonderful day.

Poem written by: Crystal da rock/ Yehuwdiyth Y. Yisrael.

THE INNER YOU

The inner you.

Is the real you.

It's the truth; that no matter what you say, think, or do, will cannot change
that fact.

Again, the inner
you should be
priority.

And I say that; this is because that's the reality.

And, besides that,
The inner you are the one that keeps you going, that keeps you up; also,
that really gets you through.

For without the inner you, there would be
nothing that you could do.

But,

to just watch everything that goes around you; see everyone; everything that surrounds you in hopelessness.

And what I mean by that, is this...
That you must keep in mind that the true-life force is from within, and the fire, the electricity; the drive and passion to live; for life is from within; not from the outside.

In a nutshell,
It is the spirit from within; that is really you deep down inside that is really running things, it's the actual being.
And that's from the very beginning and at the very end.

In fact, picture this,
The inner man, you, are like the engine in a car.

Yep! I know it may sound bizarre.

But, at the end of the day,
The inner you are what will be left standing, standing up; tall through it all.

And that's whether you realize it or not. It is what it is.

Just keep in mind love, that the real you (the inner you) are not the outfit that you are wearing on the outside, but that it is the core to; of everything; of everyone.

And remember that the inner man, you are where your focus; attention should be the most.

For without it, you, we would end up having nothing that is meaningful.

And so, show some love to you: meaning to your inner self first and foremost. For everything else is secular.

Anyway, be good to yourself; allow yourself to be good to someone else.

Shalom.

Praise Love, the Gods, and the Goddesses of Love and of righteousness always and forevermore.

Poem written by: Crystal da rock/Yehuwdiyth Y. Yisrael.

LOOK OUT YOUR WINDOW TODAY

Look out your window today.

And what do you see?

Did you see a beautiful day?

Even though the sun didn't come out to play.

And to show its amazing, and blazing sun rays.

Again, I say, look out your window today.

And, again, I ask what do you see?

Did you see the birds flying around; also, singing, or chirping?

And did you see that the grass was still green?

And did you see some beautiful beings? traveling, moving, gazing; or simply just enjoying the views.

Or by the way,

Did you feel the fresh blowing wind, or breeze that was blowing out there,

and through the open windows?

Well, bottom

line,

just be grateful that you were blessed by the God of Love to have seen it

all, and the day as well.

Poem written by: Crystal da rock/Yehuwdiyth Y. Yisrael.

WATCH YOUR EVERY MOVE

Watch your every step; or moves.

Why? Because it's important to do so.

And because it will help you; or me to pay attention to our actions; also, it give us a chance to self-monitor ourselves; also to help you, us to take the time to discern if we're going, doing; or seeing right, or wrong.

And so, with that, I say be positive, be patient, be productive; also, be vigilant and be strong.

Folks, I say this and that,

because it was my Heavenly Father,

Mr. Love Himself, that said to me to focus and to take; make note of my actions just so I can see clearly; to be able to keep record of myself in check in order to see which direction that I am heading to, which is right or wrong; or am I doing bad, or good years ago.

And believe me, I am grateful to him for that.

It's just such a relief to know and to see that it works; it helps too.

In fact, I will forever be thankful; also, grateful for and to my Heavenly parents period for the love, wisdom, knowledge and for the divine understanding that they blessed me with, right along with my twin sister, Abiygayil C. Yisrael.

So, loves in a nutshell,

Always seek to pay attention to your every move that you make; or to every steps that you take; or to every word that you speak closely; carefully with the intent to learn, correct and to grow from it all.

Shalom; praise the Gods and the Goddesses of Love and of righteousness always and forevermore.

Poem written by: Crystal da rock/ Yehuwdiyth Y. Yisrael

A GLASS HOUSE

A glass house.

It's a house; or a mind that is very transparent.

It's a house that stands on something solid although it's clear as glass.

And, I called it a glass house, not because it is weak, but it is, because it's

a house, a mind; or family; or a household that has nothing to hide; nor

can it be broken; or be divided through bribes, deceits or lies.

And that there is one powerful glass house that stands like a brick house;

but that is extremely transparent as a glass.

Bottom line, I say,

Admire the transparency; enjoy the longevity; the solidity that this house

brings and that it is manifesting right before our very eyes; wow... what a

surprise.

For it is not every glass house that can easily be broken inside or out.

And, it's simply, because it keeps all weaknesses; or all possible weaknesses on the outskirts; yet, while, standing up with all stoutness and with no doubt.

Shalom.

Poem written by: Crystal da rock/ Yehuwdiyth Y. Yisrael.

GO AND SMELL THE ROSES

Go and smell the roses today.

Get up and strike a pose; make up your mind to go and smell the roses today.

Why? Because it's time to do so.

Even though you had a hard time, a struggling moment; some torments, still rise and shine and go smell the roses today, because life goes on, and because happiness is to be gotten.

And that's an order, even though, you may feel rotten deep down inside.

Still, I say be grateful to be alive; be thankful that you survived the ups and the downs of life.

For there is always a silver lining that is always there hidden in the midst of it all; or in the atmosphere.

And so with that being said, have no fear and go out and still smell the

roses today.

Because there is still fresh air, hope, and a life to live one way or another.

So, put a smile on your face, spruce up and believe that there will be

better days ahead no matter what; know that there is still a God above that

possesses a whole lot of love for you and me.

And so, be hopeful and continue to pray, and to go out and smell the

roses, because life isn't over; nor is that your final destination.

LOL...

But, anyway, as I close out, I will say thank God for life; also, for his roses

that he blessed us to be able to smell.

LOL...

Well, bottom line, what I meant is that,

Let us keep on enjoying the gift of life even after some disappointments, sadness; or after some madness, because life is a gift that keeps on giving; that gives us hope to keep on living with the expectations that there is and will always be something good to come; or to inhale even if it's the roses at the end.

Shalom, shalom.

Poem written by: Crystal da rock/ Yehuwdiyth Y. Yisrael.

PLANT YOUR SEEDS

Plant your seeds

In a place that is good, rich and right.

And you will end up reaping the seeds of life, love and light with a delight.

And so, keep in mind that,

Your seeds will not only comes out to be good, because of where you

planted it only, but it will be good, because you first wanted a good, rich

and righteous seeds.

Hey! Remember if the seeds are planted on good grounds, it will take,

grow, and sprout with no doubt.

Right?! LOL....

Well, anyway, whatever that you plant, let it be a blessing unto you; to all

else.

Shalom.

Poem written by: Crystal da rock/ Yehuwdiyth Y. Yisrael.

<u>REPENT</u>

Repent.

It's a way, a system; or a method to reflect and not to accept defeat.

It's something that we ought to consider to do, to help ourselves escape

the woes to come.

In fact,

It's a way to reconnect by to the Creator above.

Also,

Repenting is a real beautiful thing.

By the way,

It will keep the stings of many plagues at bay; hopefully not comes your

way.

But hey.... just keep in mind that, with repentance comes confessions,

being prayed up; the turning away from your; of our sinful thoughts, ways,

and wrongful dealings.

Bottom line,

Repenting is a way to help us feel better, shine brighter and to do greater

in the sight of the Almighty God, YAHWA, YHWH, Mr. Himself.

So, loves if we wants to see a smile on our Heavenly Father face, then let's

begin and end with repenting of our sins; working on sinning no more with

sincerity within our core.

So, shalom; praise and raise the name of the God of Love forevermore and

eternally.

Poem written by: Crystal da rock/ Yehuwdiyth Y. Yisrael

DANGER IS AHEAD

Danger is ahead

If your dead in the head.

And, I mean if you're mentally blind; or spiritually lacking; behind in the

discernment of noticing right from wrong, is and will be a danger for you,

me; or for anyone that is mentally trap, or captured by illusions,

deceptions and by the misconceptions of this ungodly world.

And so, do some soul searching, analyzing and reflecting.

Further,

Do pay attention to the signs; to the times

That is coming; as well, to the developments that is taking place right

under your noses; also, right in your face.

And so, with that being said,

Seek to wake up my people to what really matters the most which is the truth, God and your precious peace of mind, that is much more valuable than anything else.

In fact, I say that, because danger is ahead, for those of us who thinks that our safety is the world; or in the materials; or in the possessions that we own.

But, my dear loves, none of these things can save us; or can help deliver us.

Bottom line,

Keep in mind that the danger ahead is actually not being connected to the Creator above, for he is our fortress and our refuge in all circumstances.

So be sure that you are not in the danger zone standing all alone.

In fact, my loves, I will say this, let us

Stay prayed up, turn from our wicked ways; as well, and seek the face of The Almighty God, Mr. Love Himself; so, we will be able to stand and to endure the upcoming dangers ahead with a peace of mind; with

convictions within our spirit that we are not alone, because he is there for

us no matter what it looks like around us; or among us.

And so, let us put our trust in him who can get us through it all with love

and serenity.

Shalom.

Poem written by: Crystal da rock/ Yehuwdiyth Y. Yisrael.

STAY FOCUS ON THE MOST HIGH

Stay focus on the most high.

Because he is the one that will always be there, here and be everywhere

with you and me.

Also, it is, because at the end of the day, when all fails, the most high God

and king, will be the one who sees us through; that will help keep us up

throughout the good, the bad and throughout the ugly one way or another.

And so, with that being said,

Glory be to the most high God, Mr. Love Himself always and eternally.

For he is our fortress and our refuge in our times of difficulties and in our

times of need and in distress.

All in all, let us all put our trust in him, our Father in Heaven, and not in

men.

For he is the one that will not abandon us; nor jump ship on us.

Shalom.

Poem written by: Crystal da rock/ Yehuwdiyth Y. Yisrael.

REAL TALK

Real talk.

Manifest real actions.

Without the distractions.

Bottom line,

Real talk holds much more clout when it is demonstrated by; through real

steps, sincere movements and dedicated foot works.

So, at the end of the day,

Let your talk and walk goes hard and hand all the way around.

Or let your words be your bond.

And now that's real talk.

LOL...

For it is your works that validates you, or the things that you talk always.

Hey! Keep in mind that, that is what will make the good LORD, YAHWA,

Mr. Love Himself, happy; not snappy.

So, shalom loves; let's keep it real and righteous in our walks in life.

Praise Love, the Gods and the Goddesses of Love and of righteousness always and forevermore from the core.

Poem written by: Crystal da rock/ Yehuwdiyth Y. Yisrael.

THE SUN RISES

The sun rises - up

Over us all; that's whether we are big or small, or short or tall.

And that there is truly a blessing for us all, to be able to see, feel; or to

experience it all in all.

Boy! I tell you that, that the God above is an awesome God, King; a

beautiful provider; for that we ought to be grateful; also, to be thankful as

well.

But, anyway, besides that,

The sun rises up over everything is the magnificent work; the power of the

most high.

And, believe me, it rises to take care of business in all places, spaces and

under any cases ; making all faces glowing; shinning; plus to make all

races happy, delightful and content; even very insightful thru its light and dynamite fiery rays.

For when it comes out, it comes out to shine it's delightful light on all things, beings and in areas that was not made visible; or that was hiding in the dark.

And so, with that being said,

Let us be Happy for this amazing gift that we are blessed with from the King of the universe with love in our hearts. For the sun rises to benefit us all in one way; or another.

Always keep in mind that the sun rises up to take care a lot of things that we are aware of; most definitely is unaware of too; I say that, because it will gives us something else, or another option to think about; also, to help us recognize that there is always a mystery in everything that the Creator above only knows; sees.

LOL....

I laughed because it tickles me to hear; to know that this is very powerful;

it's truly is divine.

If anything it even blows my mind.

LOL....

Shalom loves; enjoy your day and the sunrise always with a smile on your
faces.
Praise Love, the God of Love always; furthermore.

Poem written by: Crystal da rock/ Yehuwdiyth Y. Yisrael.

Made in the USA
Columbia, SC
19 November 2024

47010723R00039